C000242041

THE
ROCKY
GUIDE TO
LIFE

RUNNING PRESS
PHILADELPHIA · LONDON

9 8 7 6 5 4 3 2 1
Digit on the right indicates the number of this printing

Library of Congress Control Number: 2006930899

ISBN 978-0-7624-2959-2

Cover design by Joshua McDonnell
Interior design by Joshua McDonnell & Susan Van Horn
Edited by Jennifer Leczkowski
Typography: Aachen, Antique Olive, Alternate Gothic, Boton, Bulldog, Franklin Gothic, Goudy, Helvetica, and Popla

This book may be ordered by mail from the publisher.
Please include $2.50 for postage and handling.
But try your bookstore first!

Running Press Book Publishers
125 South Twenty-second Street
Philadelphia, Pennsylvania 19103-4399

Visit us on the web!
www.runningpress.com

CONTENTS

INTRODUCTION	4
PERSEVERANCE	6
WISDOM	34
DEDICATION	68
CONFIDENCE	90
OPTIMISM	114

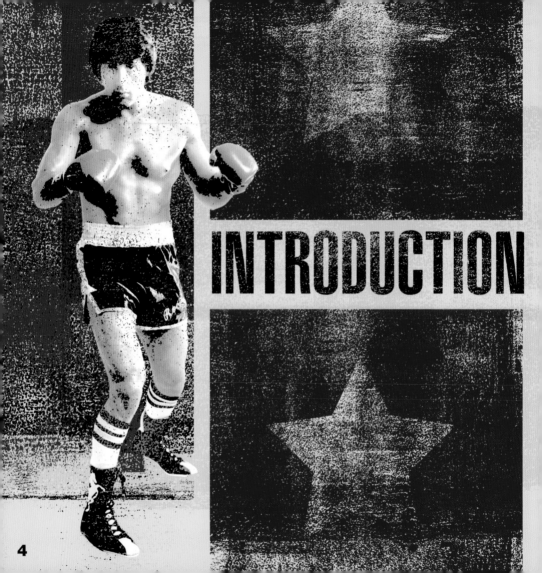

INTRODUCTION

In 1976, the world was introduced to one of the most memorable and inspiring characters in American film. Much more than just a boxing movie, the original *Rocky*, and the five sequels that followed, is an evocative depiction of the great American values of courage, determination, and the will to "go the distance."

Rocky Balboa, a down-and-out Philadelphia club fighter and part-time leg breaker, is offered a once-in-a-lifetime opportunity to fight the undefeated Heavyweight Champion of the World, Apollo Creed. By offering the local underdog "Italian Stallion" a chance at the world title, Apollo believes the fight will give audiences what they want to see—an opportunity for a "nobody" to succeed in the face of unbeatable odds. Rocky doesn't win the fight, but proves himself when he refuses to stay down and battles through fifteen rounds until the final bell rings.

This fight and the lessons Rocky learns set the stage for the subsequent films, in which he wins the belt and challenges a series of colorful opponents: Apollo Creed, Clubber Lang, Ivan Drago, Tommy Gunn, Mason Dixon . . . and ultimately, himself.

Now you can learn some a few things from Rocky and his menacing opponents—as well as Mick and Adrian!—with this collection of the best quotations from the *Rocky* series paired with some of the most unforgettable images from all six films.

PERSEVERANCE

ITALIAN STALLION

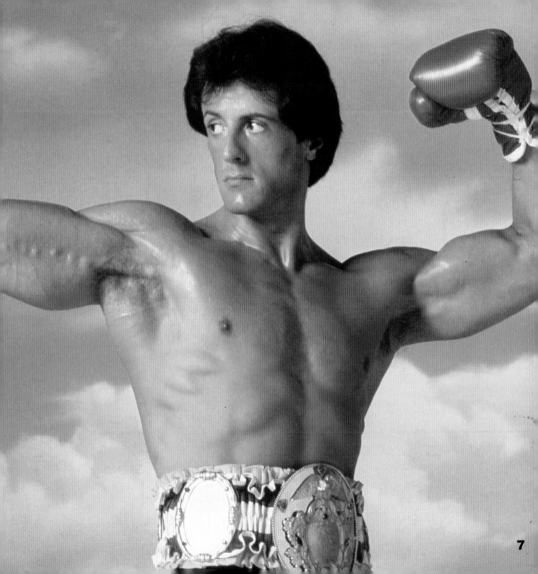

7

GO

THE

DISTANCE

- Rocky

WHAT'S CAN'T?

THERE AIN'T NO CAN'TS!

★★★★★

— Mick

10

IT AIN'T ABOUT
HOW HARD YOU HIT,
IT'S ABOUT
HOW MUCH YOU CAN TAKE AND
KEEP GOIN'.

-Rocky

13

SPEED!

— Mick

It's **ALL HEART,** you understand? It ain't all muscle, **IT'S ALL HEART.**

— Rocky

DON'T GIVE UP.

GET THAT OLIVE OIL OUT OF YOU!

• Mick

YOU GOTTA GET THAT LOOK BACK, ROCK.

EYE OF THE TIGER, MAN. - Apollo

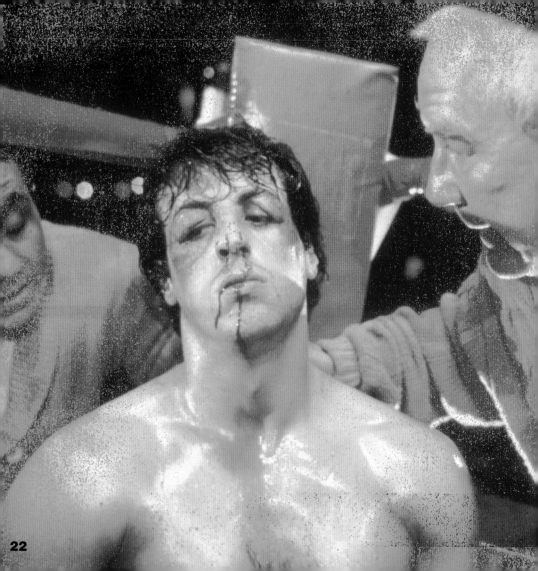

YOU AIN'T GONNA GET A

2nd CHANCE

- Mick

THINGS GET PRETTY TOUGH

IN THE RING

— Rocky

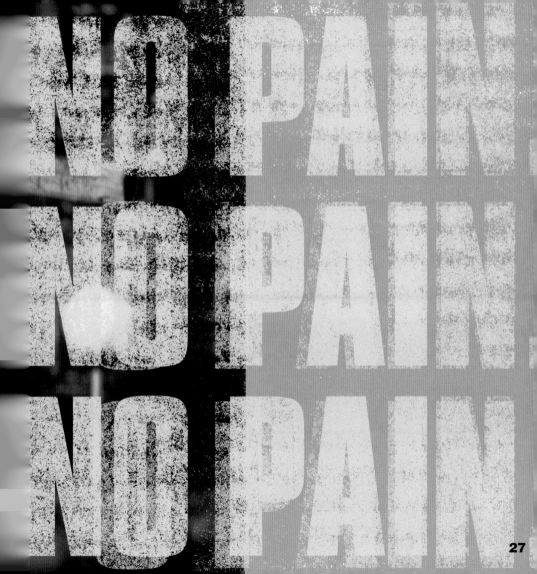

NO PAIN. NO PAIN. NO PAIN.

YOU OR NOBODY AIN'T NEVER GONNA

HIT AS HARD AS LIFE.

– Rocky

NOW GET UP.

ONE MORE ROUND.

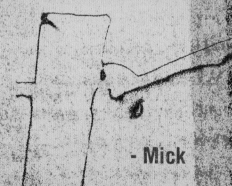

- Mick

YO, ADRIAN! I DID IT!

— Rocky

WISDOM

APOLLO CREED

THE MASTER OF DISASTER

PAY THE MAN.

YOU WANNA BORROW, YOU GOTTA PAY THE MAN.

- Rocky

YOU KNOW, MICK USED TO SAY A FIGHT AIN'T OVER 'TIL YOU HEARD THE BELL.

– Rocky

HEY, SOME PEOPLE GOT THEIR HEADS ON BACKWARDS.

– Rocky

YOU WANNA DANCE,
YOU GOTTA PAY THE BAND
UNDERSTAND?

- Rocky

I THINK PEOPLE DIE SOMETIMES WHEN THEY DON'T WANT TO LIVE NO MORE.

AND NATURE IS SMARTER THAN PEOPLE THINK.

- Mick

YOU HANG OUT WITH

YO-YO

PEOPLE

YOU GET

YO-YO FRIENDS.

— Rocky

YEAH, BUT YOU THINK YOU OUGHTA
STOP TRYING THINGS BECAUSE YOU
HAD TOO MANY BIRTHDAYS?

I DON'T.

~ Rocky

HEY, CRIME DON'T PAY.

– Rocky

RUN FOR YOUR LIFE!

— Mick

NOBODY OWES NOBODY NOTHIN'.
YOU OWE YOURSELF.

— Rocky

YOU WANNA GO OUT IN STYLE, YOU WANNA GO OUT IN ONE PIECE.

— Mick

PATIENCE

IS A

VIRTUE,

YOU KNOW?

— Rocky

THE WORST THING HAPPENED TO YOU
THAT CAN HAPPEN TO ANY FIGHTER.
YOU GOT CIVILIZED.

-Mick

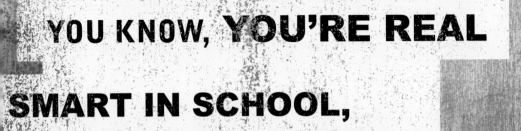

YOU KNOW, **YOU'RE REAL** SMART IN SCHOOL, BUT YOU GOTTA **BE SMART** **ON THE STREET,** TOO, SEE?

- Rocky

I JUST GOTTA DO WHAT I GOTTA DO.

— Rocky

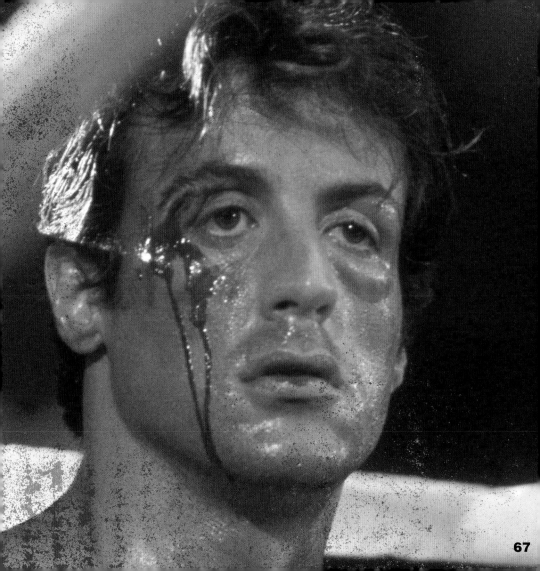

ATTON

CLUBBER LANG
THE SOUTHSIDE SLUGGER

DON'T BE A SLACKER

~ Mick

YOU LIVE SOMEPLACE LONG ENOUGH,

YOU ARE
THAT PLACE.

— Rocky

74

I'M WITH YOU,
NO MATTER WHAT.

- Adrian

JUST KEEP PUNCHIN'

- Rocky

YOU SEE YOURSELF DOING RIGHT, AND YOU DO RIGHT!

— MICK

WE'VE BEEN DOWN BEFORE . . .

WE JUST

GOTTA STICK TOGETHER.

— Rocky

TEND TO BUSINESS, WILL YA!

–Mick

BECAUSE IF YOU LOVE SOMEBODY, YOU LIVE WITH THEM. YOU DON'T GAMBLE WITH A LIFE.

- Adrian

IT DON'T HURT
HAVING AN
ANGEL
IN
YOUR CORNER,
YOU KNOW?

- Rocky

CONFIDENCE

IVAN DRAGO

DRAGO

THE SIBERIAN BULL

I MUST BREAK YOU

-Drago

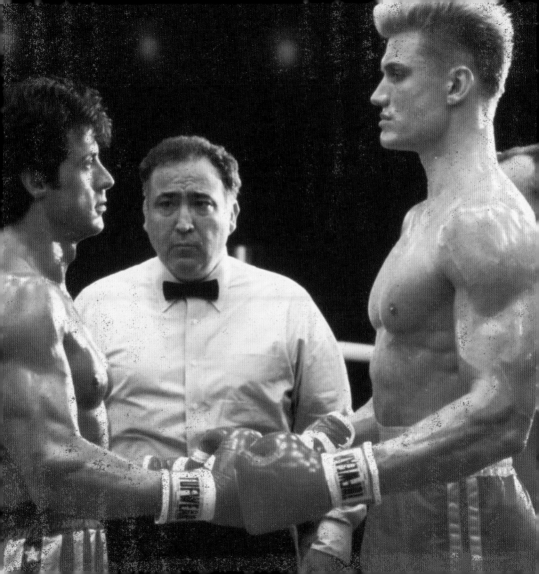

NOTHING IS REAL IF YOU DON'T

BELIEVE IN
WHO YOU ARE!

- Rocky

HE CAN RUN, BUT HE CAN'T HIDE.

- Clubber Lang

THERE'S NOTHING WRONG WITH BEING AFRAID.

- Adrian

MAYBE THE SHOW IS OVER

- Rock

IT TAKES A HELL OF A MAN TO CHANGE, BUT YOU DID IT AND YOU'RE GONNA PROVE IT.

-Apollo

MICK USED TO SAY THE ONLY **DIFFERENCE BETWEEN A HERO AND A COWARD** IS THE

HERO'S WILLING TO GO FOR IT, WILLING TO TAKE THE SHOT.

– Rocky

I PITY THE FOOL

– Clubber Lang

WHY DO YOU WANNA GO BACK TO THE SAME PLACE YOU STARTED FROM?

—Rocky

I FIGHT
TO WIN

- Drago

IF YOU KNOW WHAT YOU'RE WORTH,

THEN GO OUT

AND GET

WHAT YOU'RE WORTH

- Rocky

OPTIMISM

GOING IN
ONE MORE ROUND

WHEN YOU DON'T THINK YOU CAN—
THAT'S WHAT

MAKES ALL
THE DIFFERENCE
IN YOUR LIFE

—Rocky

ANYONE WHO'S GOT TWO FISTS, RIGHT, AND A GOOD HEARTBEAT, HAS GOT A CHANCE.

- Rocky

GO FOR IT!

YOU CAN BE WHATEVER YOU WANT TO BE.

-Adrian

121

WE NEED A FEW LAUGHS IN OUR LIFE.

— Rocky

IN HERE WE'RE TWO GUYS

KILLING EACH OTHER,

BUT I GUESS THAT'S BETTER

THAN 20 MILLION.

- Rocky

IF I CAN CHANGE,
— AND —
YOU CAN CHANGE,

EVERYBODY
CAN CHANGE

— Rocky